Wangari Maathai

Terry Barber

WOMEN
WHO
INSPIRE

Wangari Maathai is published by
Grass Roots Press, a division of Literacy Services of Canada Ltd.
www.grassrootsbooks.net

ACKNOWLEDGEMENTS

We acknowledge the financial support of the Government of Canada through the Canada Book Fund (CBF) for our publishing activities. **Canadä**

Produced with the assistance of the Government of Alberta through the Alberta Multimedia Development Fund. *Alberta*

Editor: Dr. Pat Campbell
Image research: Dr. Pat Campbell
Book design: Lara Minja

Library and Archives Canada Cataloguing in Publication

Barber, Terry, date
       Wangari Maathai / Terry Barber.

ISBN 978–1–77153–189–4 (paperback)

1. Maathai, Wangari. 2. Women Nobel Prize winners—
Kenya—Biography. 3. Women environmentalists—Kenya—
Biography. 4. Women politicians—Kenya—Biography.
5. Kenya—Biography. 6. Readers for new literates. I. Title.

PE1126.N43B36787 2016   428.6'2   C2016–906607–X

Printed in Canada.

Contents

A hummingbird in the forest.

The Hummingbird Story

The bird is tiny. The bird can fly fast. The bird's wings beat fast. The bird's wings hum when it flies. We call the bird a hummingbird. Wangari loves to tell the story of the hummingbird.

A hummingbird beats its wings from 10 to 80 times per second.

A deer watches the fire.

The Hummingbird Story

The forest is on fire. The forest
animals are afraid. The animals
watch the fire burn the forest. The
hummingbird does not watch. The
hummingbird acts. The hummingbird
flies over the fire. From its beak falls
a drop of water.

The hummingbird finds water.

The Hummingbird Story

The hummingbird flies to the stream.
It takes another drop of water. The
hummingbird flies over the fire, again
and again. Each time, a drop of water
falls from its beak. The fire burns on.
Is the hummingbird wasting its time?

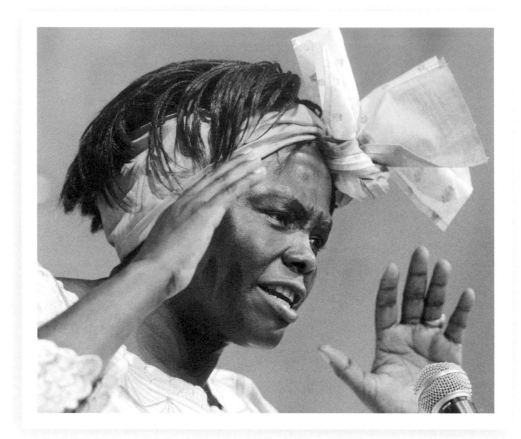

Wangari tells her story.

The Hummingbird Story

What if the other animals help? If they work together, they can put out the fire. The hummingbird shows them how. But knowing how isn't the same as doing. Wangari's story **inspires** people to do the best they can.

Africa

Wangari is born in Ihithe, a village in Kenya.

Early Years

Wangari is born in 1940. She is born in Kenya. Wangari has five brothers and sisters. Wangari's family farms the land. The land gives them all they need. Wangari's parents work hard. The family never goes hungry.

A Kikuyu village in Nyeri District.

Early Years

The land is green and healthy. The weather is the same year after year. The farmers know when the rains come. The farmers know when the drier months come. The families have enough clean water to drink.

Wangari's family belongs to the Kikuyu tribe.

Left to right: Wangari's mother, Wangari's aunt, Wangari.

1993.

Wangari's Education

Wangari is a smart child. Her parents want her to dream. Her parents want her to be creative.

Wangari is close to her mother. Wangari is proud that she and her mother never argue. Wangari's mother teaches Wangari to respect the land.

Most parents send only their boys to school.

Wangari's Education

Wangari's oldest brother asks his mother: "How come Wangari doesn't go to school?" Wangari's mother thinks for a minute. Then she says: "There's no reason why not." Wangari is sent to school. She is eight years old.

Females are treated like second-class citizens.

These nuns are Wangari's teachers.

Wangari's Education

The teachers are nuns. They help to shape Wangari's life. They inspire Wangari to help those in need. Wangari learns that everyone deserves justice. Wangari finishes high school in 1959. She loves to learn. She wants to go to college.

Wangari gets a **scholarship** to study in the United States.

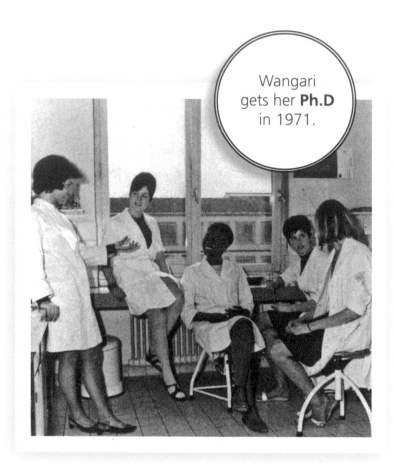

Wangari
gets her **Ph.D**
in 1971.

Wangari goes to university.

Wangari's Education

Wangari moves to the U.S. in 1960.
She studies **biology** for five years.
Wangari returns to Kenya. She falls
in love and marries in 1969. Wangari
teaches at a university in Kenya. Life is
good, but Kenya is changing.

A **clear-cut** forest.

Wangari's Work

Wangari's work takes her into poor rural areas. She is shocked to see the land. The earth is naked. People cut down the trees for firewood. Rain carries the topsoil into rivers. Tea and coffee now grow where forests once stood.

The government wants the people to grow **cash crops**.

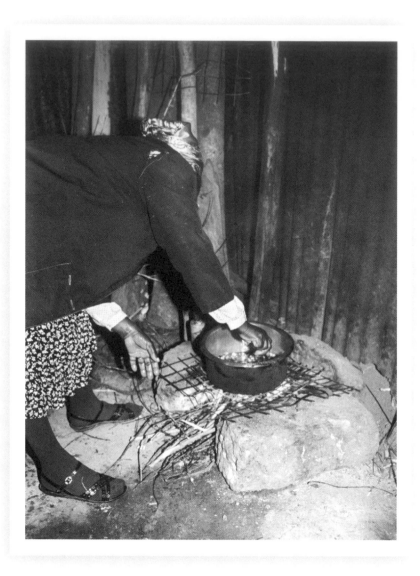

This woman uses firewood to cook.

Wangari's Work

Wangari sees that people are hungry. People cannot live on tea and coffee. They also need firewood and clean water. Wangari wants to help the people. She asks herself: "What shall I do?" An idea comes to her. "Why not plant trees?"

Wangari gives a woman a tree to plant.

Wangari's Work

Planting trees is the answer. Trees give shade to people and animals. Trees hold soil in place. Fruit trees give people food. The wood from trees makes good fences. Dead trees make good firewood.

Up to 85% of rural Africans use firewood for cooking and heating.

A girl plants a row of trees.

Wangari's Vision

Wangari's plan to plant trees is called
the Green Belt Movement (GBM).
This movement pays poor women to
plant trees. Farm women plant trees.
Schoolgirls plant trees. Church women
plant trees. Wangari brings hope to
the women.

The GBM
is formed
in 1977.

Wangari and her husband, Mwangi, in 1971.

Wangari's Vision

In 1977, Wangari's life changes. Her husband wants a divorce. He thinks Wangari is too hard to control. The divorce becomes public. Wangari hears the lies. *"She cheats on her husband."* *"She is cruel."* These lies hurt her good name.

Wangari's husband files for divorce in 1979.

Wangari talks to women about planting trees.

Wangari's Vision

In 1982, Wangari decides to leave the university. She wants to enter politics. But the government stops her. Wangari has no job and no money. She loses her home. But she never loses her vision. The Green Belt Movement spreads.

The GBM plants 51 million trees between 1978 and 2016.

Wangari leads a dance with women from the GBM.

Wangari's Vision

Planting a tree is a simple thing to do. But it makes the women feel more confident. The GBM helps women stand up for their rights. The GBM helps women stand up for the rights of the land.

Wangari leads a protest.

Wangari's Vision

The government wants to build a tower in a park. Wangari writes **protest** letters. The women in the GBM want to protect the land. The government is angry. They call Wangari crazy. The women stop the tower from being built.

In 1989, the government wants to build a 60-storey tower in Uhuru Park.

Wangari is carried to a hospital after she was beaten.

Wangari's Vision

The government tries to shut down
the GBM. But the women do not give
up. They keep fighting for the land.
Sometimes the women are beaten. But
they win many battles. The women
save many parks and forests.

The
President
says Wangari
has "insects
in her head."

Wangari answers her cell phone.

A Woman to Remember

In 2004, Wangari rides in a van with others. She answers her cell phone. The call is short. Tears roll down Wangari's cheeks. Wangari has won the Nobel Peace Prize. Now, the rest of the world will know about Wangari.

Wangari is the first African woman to win the Nobel Peace Prize.

People follow the car that holds Wangari's body.

A Woman to Remember

Wangari dies in 2011. From birth to death, Wangari never walks alone. Wangari learns from others. Wangari teaches others. In her journey, Wangari makes the earth a better place. The story of the hummingbird forever walks with Wangari.

Glossary

biology: the study of living animals and plants.

cash crop: farmed to make money. Cash crops use land that could be used to grow basic food such as rice.

clear-cut: an area where the entire forest is cut down.

inspire: to encourage somebody to do something.

Ph.D: these three letters mean Doctor of Philosophy.

protest: to complain about something.

scholarship: a payment to support a student's education.

Talking About the Book

What lessons does the hummingbird story teach us?

What did you learn about the Green Belt Movement?

Why do you think the movement is called *Green Belt*?

What challenges did Wangari face during her life?

How did Wangari make the world a better place?

Picture Credits